Alaska

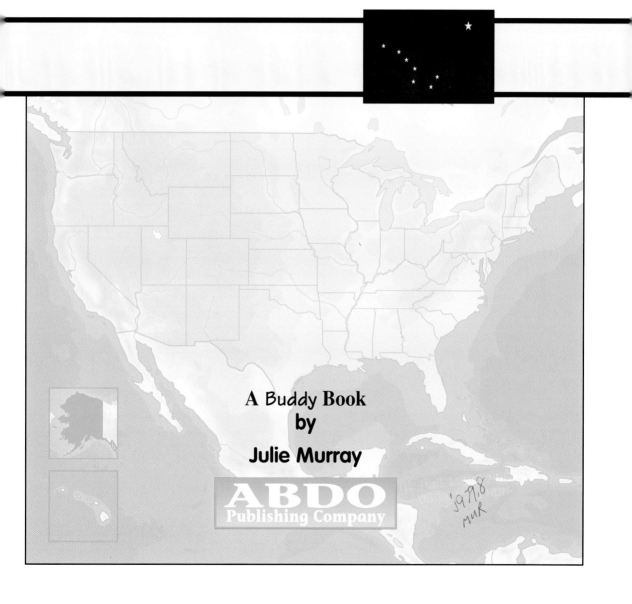

A Buddy Book
by
Julie Murray

ABDO
Publishing Company

j979.8
MUR

VISIT US AT
www.abdopub.com

EH ₽

Published by ABDO Publishing Company, 4940 Viking Drive, Edina, Minnesota 55435.

Printed in the United States.

Edited by: Sarah Tieck
Contributing Editor: Michael P. Goecke
Graphic Design: Deb Coldiron, Maria Hosley
Image Research: Sarah Tieck
Photographs: Corel, Getty Images, Medio Images, One Mile Up, PhotoDisc, Photos.com

Library of Congress Cataloging-in-Publication Data

Murray, Julie, 1969-
     Alaska / Julie Murray.
         p. cm. — (The United States)
     Includes bibliographical references and index.
     ISBN 1-59197-661-8
         1. Alaska—Juvenile literature. [1. Alaska.] I. Title.

F904.3.M88 2005
979.8—dc22

2003070814

Table Of Contents

A Snapshot Of Alaska

Alaska is the 49th state. It became an official state on January 3, 1959. Alaska was the first new state in about 47 years.

This is the summit of Mount McKinley.

Every state has an official state nickname. Alaska's state nickname is "The Last Frontier." This is because much of Alaska is wilderness. The highest mountain peak in North America is there. It is Mount McKinley at 20,320 feet (6,194 m).

The nation's largest wildlife refuge is in Alaska, too. It is the Yukon Delta National Wildlife Refuge. Also, the nation's largest national park is Wrangell–St. Elias National Park.

Alaska is the largest state in the United States. The entire state is 587,878 square miles (1,522,596 sq km).

The population of Alaska is 626,932 people.

Where Is Alaska?

There are four parts of the United States. Each part is called a region. Each region is in a different area of the country. The United States Census Bureau says the four regions are the Northeast, the South, the Midwest, and the West.

Alaska is in the West region of the United States. The weather in Alaska is cool. Sometimes it gets very cold there. This is because part of Alaska is in the Arctic. The Arctic is a very cold part of the world.

Four Regions of the United States of America

ALASKA

WASHINGTON

MONTANA

NORTH DAKOTA

OREGON

IDAHO

WYOMING

SOUTH DAKOTA

MINNESOTA

WISCONSIN

MICHIGAN

VERMONT

MAINE

NEW HAMPSHIRE

MASSACHUSETTS

NEW YORK

RHODE ISLAND

CONNECTICUT

NEVADA

UTAH

COLORADO

NEBRASKA

IOWA

ILLINOIS

INDIANA

OHIO

PENNSYLVANIA

NEW JERSEY

DELAWARE

Washington D.C.

MARYLAND

CALIFORNIA

KANSAS

MISSOURI

WEST VIRGINIA

VIRGINIA

KENTUCKY

NORTH CAROLINA

ARIZONA

NEW MEXICO

OKLAHOMA

ARKANSAS

TENNESSEE

SOUTH CAROLINA

MISSISSIPPI

ALABAMA

GEORGIA

TEXAS

LOUISIANA

FLORIDA

HAWAII

	West		Midwest		South		Northeast

Alaska is separate from most parts of the United States. It is in the northern part of North America. Most of Alaska is bordered by water. The Arctic Ocean is north. The Bering Sea is to the west. The Pacific Ocean and the Gulf of Alaska lie to the south. The country of Canada is to the east.

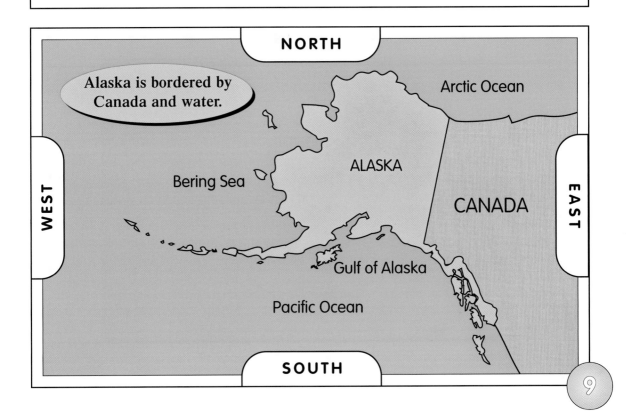

Alaska is bordered by Canada and water.

NORTH

WEST

EAST

SOUTH

Arctic Ocean

Bering Sea

ALASKA

CANADA

Gulf of Alaska

Pacific Ocean

Alaska

State abbreviation: **AK**

State nickname: The Last Frontier

State capital: Juneau

State motto: "North to the Future"

Statehood: January 3, 1959, 49th State

Population: 626,932, ranks 48th

State flag: Adopted in 1927

Land area: 587,878 square miles (1,522,596 sq km), ranks 1st

State tree: Sitka spruce

State song: "Alaska's Flag"

State government: Three branches: legislative, executive, and judicial

Average July temperature: 55°F (13°C)

Average January temperature: 5°F (-15°C)

State land mammal:
Moose

State flower:
Forget-me-not

State bird:
Willow Ptarmigan

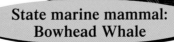
State marine mammal:
Bowhead Whale

Cities And The Capital

Juneau is the capital of Alaska. It is the second-largest city in the state. It is in the southern part of Alaska. People cannot drive cars to Juneau. This is because it is in the wilderness and surrounded by water. People can fly into the city on an airplane. Some ride ferry boats.

A view of Juneau.

Anchorage is Alaska's largest city. It has a population of 260,283 citizens. Many businesses are located in Anchorage. Oil, railroads, and military bases helped this city grow.

A view of Anchorage.

Fairbanks is the third-largest city in Alaska. Fairbanks is close to the Arctic Circle. This means it is very cold.

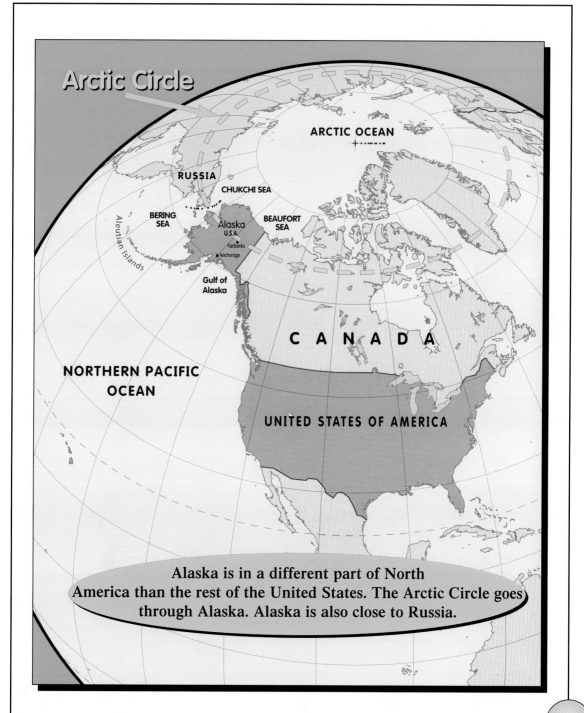

Arctic Circle

ARCTIC OCEAN

RUSSIA

CHUKCHI SEA

BERING
SEA

Aleutian Islands

Alaska
U.S.A.
Fairbanks
Anchorage

BEAUFORT
SEA

Gulf of
Alaska

NORTHERN PACIFIC
OCEAN

C A N A D A

UNITED STATES OF AMERICA

Alaska is in a different part of North
America than the rest of the United States. The Arctic Circle goes
through Alaska. Alaska is also close to Russia.

Famous Citizens

Edward Lewis "Bob" Bartlett (1904–1968)

Bob Bartlett is famous for helping to make Alaska a state. Some people call him the founding father of Alaska.

Bartlett was also one of Alaska's first United States senators. He was elected in 1959. This was the same year Alaska became a state.

Bartlett also worked as a gold miner and a newspaper reporter. He was born in Seattle, Washington. But, Bartlett moved to Fairbanks with his family when he was one year old.

Bob Bartlett

Alaska Highway

Most roads in Alaska lead to the Alaska Highway. This road is 1,397 miles (2,248 km) long. It goes from Dawson Creek, British Columbia to Delta Junction, Alaska. It is the only highway that links Alaska with other major roads in the United States and Canada.

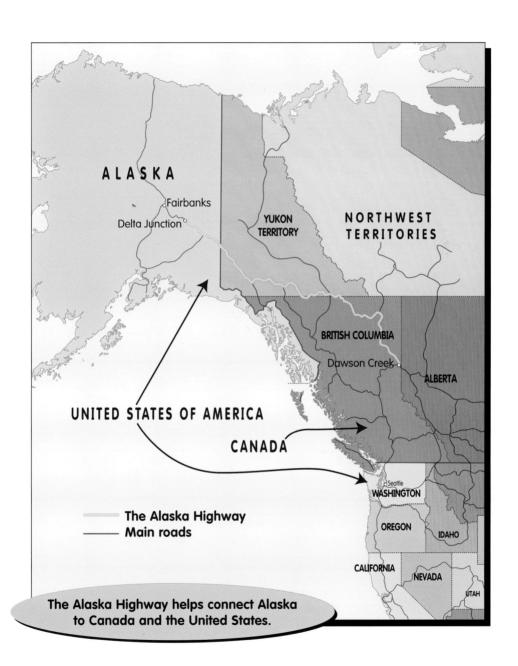

ALASKA

Fairbanks
Delta Junction

YUKON
TERRITORY

NORTHWEST
TERRITORIES

BRITISH COLUMBIA

Dawson Creek

ALBERTA

UNITED STATES OF AMERICA

CANADA

Seattle
WASHINGTON

OREGON

IDAHO

CALIFORNIA

NEVADA

UTAH

The Alaska Highway
Main roads

The Alaska Highway helps connect Alaska
to Canada and the United States.

The Alaska Highway was built in 1942 and 1943. The United States Army built this road. It was first used during World War II. At this time, it helped soldiers get supplies. Now, people use it mostly for travel.

Native People Of Alaska

Thousands of years ago, native tribes lived in Alaska. They were called Arctic people. The Arctic people were in Alaska before explorers arrived. One tribe was called Inuit. The other was called Aleut. Another group was called Yuit. Many tribe members still live in Alaska.

This woman is a member of an Inuit tribe.

Many years ago, these tribes hunted and fished for food. They used natural materials to build houses. The natural materials included animal skins, wood, and stones. They made weapons from animal bones. Boats were made out of animal skin.

Some native people in Alaska
still catch fish for food.

The tribes spoke different languages. Also, they lived in different areas. The Aleuts came from the Aleutian Islands. These islands are near the coast of Alaska. The Inuit live in the northern part of Alaska. They also live in Canada and Greenland. The Yuit settled in the south and west parts of Alaska. They also live in Russia.

The Iditarod

The Iditarod is a famous sled dog race. People drive a sled pulled by dogs. The drivers are called mushers. They must be very strong. This is because the race lasts more than nine days.

These people are driving a dogsled.

Many people come to Alaska for the Iditarod. The race happens every year on the first Saturday in March.

The race covers 1,100 miles (1,770 km) from Anchorage to Nome. The route changes every other year. Some years the racers go north. Sometimes they go south.

The Iditarod honors a historic trip. People used a dogsled to go get medicine. They drove along the same trails.

Mushers must be strong to control a team of sled dogs.

Alaska

1741: Captain Vitus Bering arrives in Alaska.

1867: The United States government buys Alaska from Russia for $7,200,000. This is about 2¢ per acre (5¢ per ha). Many people say this is a waste of money. They think Alaska is all snow. It turns out to be full of resources such as fish and oil.

Alaska is full of natural resources.

1884: Sitka is the capital of Alaska. Also, Alaska establishes laws and courts.

1897-1898: The gold rush starts in Alaska and the Klondike. The Klondike is in Canada.

1900: Juneau becomes the capital of Alaska.

1912: Alaska becomes a United States territory.

1959: Alaska becomes a state on January 3.

1964: An earthquake hits Alaska on March 27. It is one of the largest earthquakes ever in North America. This happens near Anchorage and Valdez.

1989: Oil spills in Prince William Sound. A ship named Exxon Valdez loses 11 million gallons (42 million liters) of oil. This is the largest oil spill in United States history.

Cities in Alaska

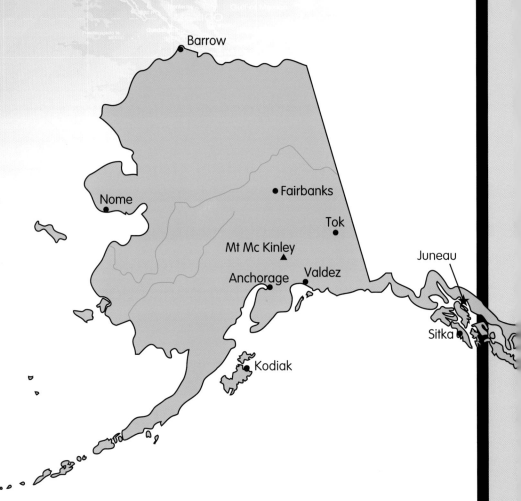

Barrow
Nome
Fairbanks
Tok
Mt Mc Kinley
Anchorage
Valdez
Juneau
Sitka
Kodiak

Important Words

Arctic the region around the North Pole.

capital a city where government leaders meet.

musher a person who drives a dogsled.

nickname a name that describes something special about a person or a place.

summit the highest point on the top of a mountain.

tribe a group of people.

wilderness land that has very few people and is covered with plants and trees.

World War II the second war between many countries that happened from 1939–1945.

Web Sites

To learn more about Alaska, visit ABDO Publishing Company on the World Wide Web. Web site links about Alaska are featured on our Book Links page. These links are routinely monitored and updated to provide the most current information available.

www.abdopub.com

Index